Lynn Xu

*

And Those Ashen Heaps
That Cantilevered
Vase of Moonlight

*

Wave Books
Seattle/New York

*

For Josh, Issa,
and Lorca

Published by Wave Books

www.wavepoetry.com

Wave Books titles are distributed to the trade by

Consortium Book Sales and Distribution

Phone: 800-283-3572 / SAN 631-760X

Library of Congress Cataloging-in-Publication Data

Names: Xu, Lynn, 1982– author.

Title: And those ashen heaps that cantilevered vase of moonlight / Lynn Xu.

Description: First edition. | Seattle : Wave Books, [2022]

Identifiers: LCCN 2021042933 | ISBN 9781950268559 (hardcover)

ISBN 9781950268542 (paperback)

Subjects: LCGFT: Poetry.

Classification: LCC PS3624.U2 A84 2022 | DDC 811/.6—dc23

LC record available at https://lccn.loc.gov/2021042933

Designed by Crisis

Printed in the United States of America

9 8 7 6 5 4 3 2 1

First Edition

Wave Books 098

AND

THOSE

ASHEN

HEAPS

THAT

CANTILEVERED

VASE

O F

MOONLIGHT

Rippling in the ceosops
foreskin of wind
still surrounded by blood
poverty
and the uneven caresses
lying at the bottom
dreaming dreaming
days of complete idleness
urinating
without rejection
transparent
at ***** in the afternoon
now rising
now setting
a windbreak of gum trees
et cetera
the edge of time
et cetera

She is floating

她漂浮着

and I float with her

我和她一起飘浮

in the middle of nothing
在没有的中间

in no shadow

在阴影的没有

The unconscious . . .
潜意识

What is it?

是什么

A voluptuousness . . . ?

一种艳色

Sun

太阳

como huevo

Before this moment

在这一刻之前

the curtain over the window

窗户上的窗帘

had been stuck

被拉住了

and the entire moon was showing

整个月亮露了出来

and then:
接着

I was born

我出生了

phosphorescing

磷光

I am born

我出生了

inside the verb which may or may not

在动词的里面可能或可能没有

have happened

发生

which may or may not be
可能或可能不是

definitive

确定

Why?
为什么

I am born . . .
我出生了

No . . .

没有

not yet

还没有

This morning

今天早上

I woke up

醒来

tied to the other side of the earth

锁在地球的另一面

The clock on the wall had stopped

墙上的钟停了

It was moving
还在移动

but several hours behind

好几个小时以后

It was midnight
半夜

noon

中午

and also midnight

和半夜

I am beginning . . .
我开始了

but this has always been true

但这一直这本身就是真的

This morning
今天早上

standing over myself

站在自己的面前

as one does

好像

a kind of poverty
一种贫穷

to be born

出生

from nothing

从没有

In the meantime
同时

I am alive

还活着

and living brings me close
活着使我接近

to everything

一切

streets . . . corpses . . . grief . . . sun

街道尸体悲伤太阳

Here in the beginning

正在开始的这里

in the first drop of blood
在第一滴血

eclipsed by a butterfly

被蝴蝶黯然失色

Today touching life
今天触摸生命

at its softest

在最柔软的

most difficult . . .

最困难的

What

什么

will people say?
怎么说

These women
这些女人

attending to my birth

帮助我的出生

on the other side of the afternoon

在下午的另一面

rising falling rising

升起落下升起

curtain

窗帘

This window I imagine
这扇窗子我想象

to be the dangerous hole

是生命打开

life opens
最危险的洞

From this first moment

从这第一瞬间

it cannot be true

不可能是真的

Today

今天

this very first moment

这第一瞬间

through which life passes
生命经过

unprotected
开始

by its beginning
无法保护

Today

今天

I touch

触摸

In the labyrinth

在一颗

of a teardrop

泪珠中迷路

on the seventeenth

十二月

of December at
十七日

six

六

no

不

seven

七点

on the verso
在日光

of the shudder

颤抖

proceeding from daylight
的反面

"Los párpados cerrados, como si,
cuando nacemos,
siempre no fuese tiempo todavía."

"Voici les morts que je vis en dernier, le dimanche, vers deux heures de l'après-midi."

"Pero el dos no ha sido nunca un número
porque es una angustia y su sombra"

Last night, beside the menstrual shadow of the corpse I saw my mother's legs (her enormous legs) opening and closing in a voluptuous trance sweeping the thick current, the amorous pity of her legs which with my mouth I imitated, still pregnant, or, became, by way of imitation, innumerable, in the meantime, her foot, her toe, which refused to dissolve, and which I could see still climbing the transparency of birth, her foot in the piedras continuing to suckle, to insist, thickness, aie-aie-aie, who is this still mothering with the rags of

a mouth, coughing and defecating in the
middle of life and continuing to urinate, in
the occultation of the middle

snow, and the grave diggers having gone,
drifted north in gusts, phalanges, nour-
ished by numbers and the supernumerary
resemblance of the turnstile, here, it is
nighttime in both directions, and in these
human temples, I attend, I dream, and I
carry my grave clothes under my arms,
mother,

with the cadavers entering childhood still
trembling like sunflowers,

I dream,

and flushed with humanity I approached
my mouth, with the vanity of the dead,
and dressed like a woman, in the path of
the coffins, foot in the piedras, living, as it
were, no more poorly than any other, with
no more blood, sperm, tears, saliva,

fungibility of the mouth,

snow,

dripping from mother, from the window,
observing the snowdrift,

and her legs (her enormous legs) opening
and closing in the thick current, which I,
with my mouth, imitated, in the mean-
time,

the corpse's one bare foot, without ped-
estal, without protection, in the ruined
street,

I,

DREAMING YOU,

FLOWING IN MY BODY,

BODY OF THE OTHER,

WRITING MYSELF,

with the illegibility of an

ALREADY that leads back to

nothing,

DON'T DIE,

as long as I am still alive,

OR,

and tonight,

having been born,

for no reason (it happens, but I am not
here),

bear with me,

it seems, I am growing less and less pre-
cise, this desire to live, to continue to live,
and without demonstration, in a night of
infinite reversals between the 1, and the 2,
and the afternoon, having established its
yesterdays,

between the poor day and the great night,
at two in the immoral afternoon,

the island swam toward me and peeled off
its dolphin skin, this legendary business
of cracking eggs with a laugh that pinches
the anus, the cloaca, the miniature coffins,
at the point where reality is, except for that
rivulet of saliva reflecting the Milky Way,
and there, in the dishpan, catch a glimpse
of you,

The un

Moth

nimous

er

When
does she

arrive?

On

Tw

o

Th

ree

Fou

r

Fi

Six

Se

ven

Eig

ght

Ni

ne

ON

THE

MINUTE

HAND

OF

TOMORROW'S

MORNING

IS

TODAY

TODAY

IN

THE

TREMENDOUS

FEAR

BETWEEN

HEAVEN AND

EARTH

TO DO

EVERYTHING

FOR THAT

WHICH DOES NOT

EXIST

stage right:

WAR OR RESISTANCE!

and the soul in tatters, what does
he do?

with his posthumous fever, his
posthumous thighs, his
posthumous foot christened by
the everlasting cartridge of night,

later on, when the family sits
down to wait for a man who has
already been shot,

stage right:

NO PURE BEGINNINGS!
AND SO ON

the aficionados,
the ones with the solid
alibis on both the left
and the right
of the moral rectum
caressing
this parallel son

HOSANNA

face with tears of joy
loudly crying face?
red heart
two hearts
face with heart eyes?
waffle?
oyster?

LIKE

THE

WAR

TO

NOURISH

YOU?

HAVE

TO

FEED

IT

SOMETHING

TOO!

Oh!
insolent
turd
competing
for the latrines
of yesterday—
all
night
long
upon the public shoulders
of the infinitesimal
inside

and yesterday
even now
the streetlamps are lit

with the destiny
of the definitive: doors
windows
foreheads
stars . . .
the newborn tongue
which struggles with its mortal
advances against the
exterminating
alphabet in the unvitiated
asylum of the moon's
pickpocket—

        why
even a bear
etc.

through the tears and fur
in the trellised
girders
of the double rainbow . . .

all
that
is
swift and
living
in the meantime
taking shape
with obvious
poverty there
being no
good and evil

only
a chain
which rattles
and resounds
in us
as bells

and as the procession
before me fled
one seemed to know
as one whose years the mask
and smokeless altars interpose
incessantly
numerous as the dead
from whose forms shadows pass
and of that great crowd
rearranged the thrush
and thrift and edelweiss: a
SHAPE whose garments in the
changing seasons as yet
formless against the
trembling like the lifting
of a veil

as in autumn-
time the leaves borne
onward by what through
eternity re-
echoes echoes
still in untilled fields the soft
and ceaseless song un-
childing un-
fathering unanimous

a SHAPE ALL LIGHT
thoroughly half-
spoken—

a singing so

to speak that
passed
through wood and
worm before
the breathless
bee

       and
having labored time-
ward through remaining
time what
over the bent world life
must borrow: that farthest-
nothing

      that incandescent

plural of the unopened
handful

there
the sun lingered

and soft as wind it passes

pure moon of the doorway

pure zero in the diadems
of the coffer's edge

the empty cart clattering

one to ten

ten to one

all things unclose
their portions

in the hour of distribution
of the balancing of accounts
and those who fight
for a few scraps of food
to renew each day unguarded
by the angels

                    at last—
all life passes
through the smiling air
windows open noiselessly

as one that in a silver
vision floats
already
decembering with the aggregate
of time's eternity—

and life
in that black or luminous
square—life
lives

repeating thriftless-
shadow
beneath the few branches
galloping through night

clear stream
                    wooden horse
blue sword

awaiting the few small acts
of cowardice still to come

from my pure throat and
the tongue close behind
I have come to trip over
the woman who has given birth,

gelatinous
contrapuntal
bamboozled, at last!
and screaming again screams
of the newborn, since she was
there also and keeps me from
my childhood,

born
born
born

orphan
with the middle eye
with brains of the butterfly
between us
plus
minus scuffed
tips shimmering in the circular
lamp, that pell-mell night-
enduring mouth:
SCRAM!
GET LOST!
PICK YOURSELF OFF!
YOU WHO GROVEL
IN THE STREET!
YOU WHO WERE BORN!

on the road
to a quivering
ZERO
prophet-
poor conspiring
I apply
exact numbers
the advancing
sovereign
spatula
and I ripen
with my virginity
where the void hustles to the
bottom

and quivering
just a little
lick my fingers
stroke the tip
and urinate
in the middle

and look at the stars

and quivering
just a little
and lick my fingers
and stroke the tip
and urinate

in the middle of the basin
and the two dippers
dipping one into the other

remember:
angels weave you
a bearded three-fourth scale
redoubled on the forehead ap-
pearing by the slow piano
of her hand

2 times 9 is eighteen

3 times 9 is twenty-seven

4 times 9 is thirty-six

5 times 9 is forty-five

6 times 9 is fifty-four

7 times 9 is sixty-three

8 times 9 is seventy-two

9 times 9 is eighty-one . . .

1 plus 8 is 9

2 plus 7 is 9

3 plus 6 is 9

4 plus 5 is 9 . . .

the hour, arranging four
bright columns beyond
the corridor of the empty child,
someone:
the fifth column,
remainder of the triangle,
advances like a bell in the afternoon

A	N	D	
E	A	S	
E	A	P	
T	C	A	
E	V	E	
A	S	E	
O	N	L	

H O S

E N H

T H A

T I L

E D V

E M O

F M O

G H T

POSTSCRIPT

and the angel
that presided over my birth
sd: [Little Creature formed of Joy]
[and Mirth] — *go Love*
without the help
of any Thing on Earth

I open my eyes as a sunflower,

the world trembles through my body, lon-
gitude, latitude, I am dancing, dancing,
dancing (born dancing!) at last: I am here
. . . in the thickness of five vertigos, the
five in the middle, like the interior of four
o'clock, or Friday, between six and seven
in the intones of the tamarind,

ta-ma-rind . . .

its green syllable un-
furls my

moon-
like
face: beautiful
in the beginning, beautiful
in the middle, beautiful
in the end

I close my eyes and open them
again within myself:
the great god
with many hands churning
churning
in a temple whose walls
are no longer there
and there
just now

is the totality
an infinitely delicate
delicateness: my birth
postponed
by the punctual inquisition
of the wheel
by all four faces
of the charioteer
and yet: I simply
think myself up! one
by one I open the doors
confronting the empty universe
for the entire duration
of the counterfeit

and the wheels

my masters
endlessly
generating:
paso
umbilical
paso
nada
tele-
pathos: passage
from cadaver
to corolla

the eyes
of the corpse
when I open them
again pure

as tiny children

I am speaking your language
without actually being
you: man,
child, justice, mercy

reality is so close,
and yet it is the point
of no return

reality: where the name eats the
body and holds it upright

now . . .
where were we? oh

yes! dancing . . .

like the procession of jewels
connecting one vow
to the other
in the splendid firmament
of time
or
the brightness it veils
throughout the double of myself

the white blossom
on the silverbell
made of tin
plate and the purest
grays of wind

it is five
by all the clocks
by all of the thirteen
cliffs
in the rectitude
of its folds
and the sprig
of asphodel
is passing
from the seller's hand

it is for you

this world,
the streets, the vinegars,

the farewells in the stations,
and the trains coming and going
with glistening windows,
the train passing with fruits
and flowers, with the oyster's
patience,
I follow the egg
into its interior,
into an afternoon
that could have been anyone's

Hello enormous sunflower sinking
back into the earth
Hello black earth
Hello to the sweetness
of nothing to mourn
of mourning nothing
the hour crossed out
invalid hour
saliva of the first letter
Hello December born
with the anxiety of January
anxiety of the meridian
of the hour before
and the hour after
hour of the pendulum
traversing midnight
denuding its numbers

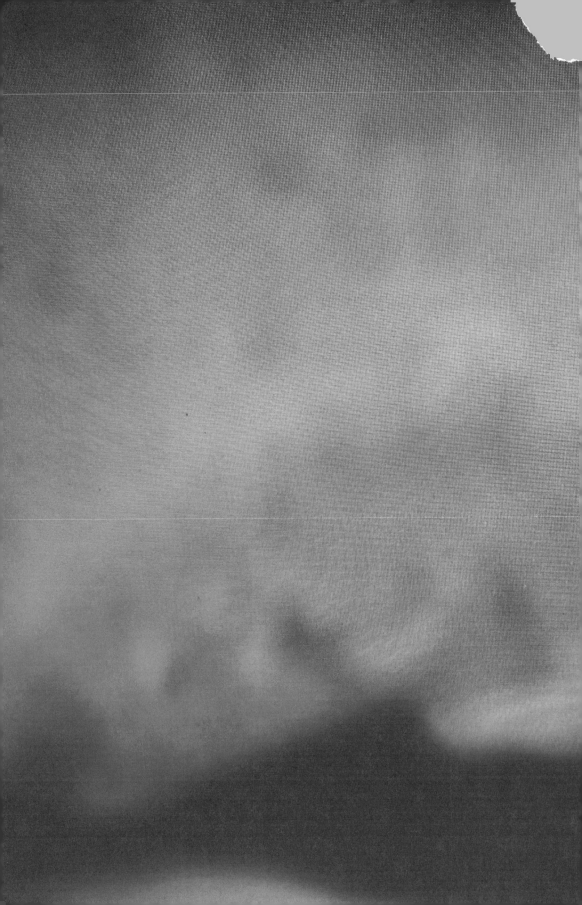

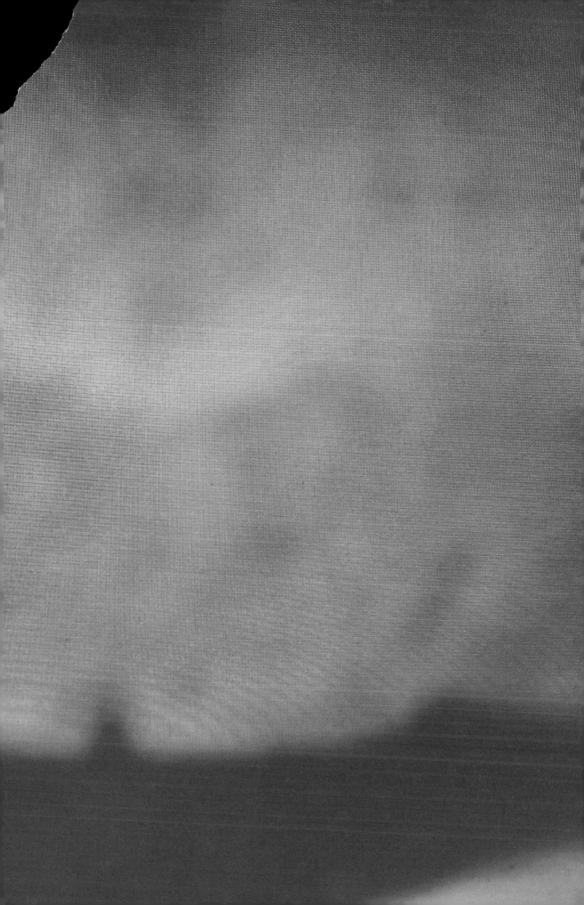

NOTES Between reading and dreaming is the mother's face ... As such, this book is filled with many mothers: Aimé Césaire, Clarice Lispector, Roland Barthes, César Vallejo, Jean Genet, Federico García Lorca, Simone Weil, Bertolt Brecht, Jorge Luis Borges, Unica Zürn, Charles Baudelaire, Arthur Rimbaud, Vladimir Mayakovsky, Percy Bysshe Shelley, Gerard Manley Hopkins, Emily Dickinson, Hilda Hilst, William Blake, Pablo Neruda, and Attila József.

ACKNOWLEDGMENTS Thank you to the curators and editors at 300 South Kelly Street, Ballroom Marfa, Cape Cod Modern House Trust, Compline, *e-flux*, the Guggenheim Museum, *Hyperallergic*, *jubilat*, the National Endowment for the Arts, *Octo 2*, Poem-a-Day, the Renaissance Society, Rising Tide Projects, and Wave Books. To my students, colleagues, friends, and family: Thank you.